W9-BMZ-351

DIG INTO ADVENTURE AROUND THE WORLD WITH...

SCIENTISTS in ACTION!

Archaeologists!

SCIENTISTS in ACTION!

Archaeologists!

Astronauts!

Big-Animal Vets!

Biomedical Engineers!

Civil Engineers!

Climatologists!

Crime Scene Techs!

Cyber Spy Hunters!

Marine Biologists!

Robot Builders!

SCIENTISTS in ACTION!

Archaeologists!

By Clifford Thompson

Mason Crest
450 Parkway Drive, Suite D
Broomall, PA 19008
www.masoncrest.com

© 2016 by Mason Crest, an imprint of National Highlights, Inc.

Printed and bound in the United States of America.

Series ISBN: 978-1-4222-3416-7
Hardback ISBN: 978-1-4222-3417-4
EBook ISBN: 978-1-4222-8478-0

First printing
1 3 5 7 9 8 6 4 2

Produced by Shoreline Publishing Group LLC
Santa Barbara, California
Editorial Director: James Buckley Jr.
Designer: Tom Carling, Carling Design Inc.
Production: Sandy Gordon
www.shorelinepublishing.com
Cover image: Kenneth Garrett

Library of Congress Cataloging-in-Publication Data

Thompson, Clifford.
　　　Archaeologists! / by Clifford Thompson.
　　　pages cm
ISBN 978-1-4222-3417-4 (hardback : alk. paper) -- ISBN 978-1-4222-3416-7 (series : alk. paper) -- ISBN 978-1-4222-8478-0 (ebook) Includes index. 1. Archaeology--Juvenile literature. I. Title.   CC171.T47 2016
930.1--dc23
　　　　　　　　　　　　　2015004022

Contents

Key Icons to Look For

Words to Understand: These words with their easy-to-understand definitions will increase the reader's understanding of the text, while building vocabulary skills.

Sidebars: This boxed material within the main text allows readers to build knowledge, gain insights, explore possibilities, and broaden their perspectives by weaving together additional information to provide realistic and holistic perspectives.

Research Projects: Readers are pointed toward areas of further inquiry connected to each chapter. Suggestions are provided for projects that encourage deeper research and analysis.

Text-Dependent Questions: These questions send the reader back to the text for more careful attention to the evidence presented here.

Series Glossary of Key Terms: This back-of-the-book glossary contains terminology used throughout this series. Words found here increase the reader's ability to read and comprehend higher-level books and articles in this field.

Action!

lana Cordy-Collins was about to make an amazing discovery. She was part of the small group from the University of California at Los Angeles (UCLA) that went on an archaeological **dig** that day in 1991. The dig took place in the village of San José de Moro, on the north coast of Peru. Machu Picchu (pictured at left) is the most famous dig in Peru. The scientists from UCLA wanted to find another important site. Cordy-Collins was an archaeologist, which meant that she often found very old items that revealed facts about long-dead people and ancient civilizations. That day, she found something she had known about for years. She had even written about it two decades earlier, for her master's degree. She just hadn't thought at the time that it was real.

WORDS TO UNDERSTAND

dig   not the verb, but the noun, which means a
   site undergoing archaeological excavation

discipline   in science, this means a particular field
   of study

Cordy-Collins's father was also an archaeologist, and as a girl she had gone on digs with him in Little Lake, California. The things they found were shown in the Southwest Museum in Los Angeles. When Alana went to UCLA, she studied art history. She was still interested in art when she got her master's degree and Ph.D. in archaeology.

Her interest in art, and her work in archaeology, had led her to Peru. "I was drawn to Peru because, at that time, the field was so wide open," she says, meaning that few people in the United States had done work in archaeology there. "We didn't even know all the questions to ask; almost anything one did was a contribution to the **discipline**."

Cordy-Collins studied paintings left behind by members of Peru's Moche (pronounced "MOH-chay") civilization. The Moche culture existed for several centuries, beginning nearly 2,000 years ago. The colored images were parts of murals or were found on objects such as ceramic bottles. Many of the paintings show priestesses, who were very powerful and important figures in the Moche society.

In the images, the priestesses were always shown wearing headdresses with two, three, or four large plumes of feathers. The headdresses often had head cloths that hung down the priestesses' backs. Often, the priestesses were shown with oval objects attached to their waists. Those objects were related to something the priestesses were shown doing in the paintings—something you might see in a horror movie.

The paintings were often about human sacrifices. The paintings showed tied-up male prisoners captured in war. The priestesses could be seen drinking from cups made from sacred shells found under water. They were actually drinking the prisoners' blood. Experts like Alana knew that the oval objects tied to the priestesses' waists were weights, used to help divers stay under water long enough to find the shells.

Cordy-Collins knew all about the paintings. She just didn't think that the people in them were real.

The site of the dig in San José de Moro was under a pen where cattle were kept. Because the site was hidden, looters had not stolen what was underneath. In order to dig at the site, Cordy-Collins and the others had to get through layers of mud and ancient brick. The easiest way to get through it would have been to use a big vehicle such as a backhoe. However, the UCLA archaeologists didn't want to damage anything valuable so they had to use small tools such as brushes, spatulas, and their own hands. The team went so deep into the ground—30 feet (9 m)—that they had to make ladders from bamboo. They hauled out the dirt in specially made, heavy-duty metal buckets attached to thick hemp rope.

Moche paintings were just part of an ancient culture's many artistic works. Located in Peru, the Moche thrived for nearly eight centuries, until about 800 CE.

This statue of another Moche princess mummy, known as the Lady of Cao, was found more than a decade after Cordy-Collins and her team made the first such discoveries in the region.

Finally, the team found tombs. One revealed the burial of a woman about 35 years of age, along with two of her female servants. By studying the fancy objects buried with them, Cordy-Collins discovered that the woman was someone she knew, but only known from Moche art. She was a priestess, just like the ones in the paintings!

The following year, returning to San José de Moro, the UCLA archaeologists found another huge chamber tomb that contained a second priestess with her servants. She was a bit younger—25 or so when she died. The archaeologist found it strange and exciting to realize that she had written about people from the past, without having any idea that they had been real.

Cordy-Collins had spent years studying archaeology. Some of her time had been spent in the classroom, but the things she learned often led her out of the classroom, to far away places where she discovered objects no one had ever seen before. The work done by Alana Cordy-Collins and others like her is hard, often exciting, and occasionally even dangerous—and it helps people understand more about the history of the world they live in.

This is the work of archaeologists.

The Scientists and Their Science

How do we know what ordinary people did hundreds and thousands of ago? Not just kings, queens, or explorers, but people like us? How do we know what they ate, what they wore, what their homes looked like, and how they decorated them? No one from those days is around to tell us, and even written records go back only so far. So we have to figure out the answers from objects that are left behind. The objects are clues, and the people who piece together the clues are like detectives. They're called archaeologists.

WORDS TO UNDERSTAND

innovative   groundbreaking, original

minors   additional large fields of study for undergraduate college students, but that do not lead to a degree in that field

paleontologists   scientists who look for, and study, ancient fossils of animals and plants

When you say the word "archaeologist," a lot of people think of Indiana Jones. He is a make-believe archaeologist from the movies, beginning with *Raiders of the Lost Ark* (1981). It seemed that every time Jones went looking for ancient objects, he ran into dangerous situations that called for him to use his fists, his pistol, or the bullwhip he always carried. Real archaeologists don't usually face quite as much danger as Indiana Jones. (If they did, they wouldn't survive.) Like Indy, though, they look for ancient objects.

An archaeologist goes on digs. Digs are what they sound like: Archaeologists and their helpers use shovels to dig up dirt and find what's

Life at a dig is not glamourous. The work of archaeologists calls for them to get into the dirt and mud, digging back through time to discover connections to humankind's past.

underneath. Sometimes, the things they find reveal a lot about people from long ago. Sometimes, the things they find are the people themselves. Bones and teeth from people who lived thousands of years ago can tell us how tall they were, how large their brains were, even what they ate.

Sometimes archaeologists dig up parts of buildings and figure out how they were made and what they were made of. Other digs turn up things such as vases. Details of a vase can show how potters worked at the time. For example, small differences between shapes of vases reveal if they were crafted by hand or made from

Decorated Greek vases provide a peek into a culture more than 2,500 years old.

a mold. Also, the way a vase is decorated can tell us what the people cared about, and reveal something about their culture. For example, some Greek vases from 2,500 years ago are decorated with characters from the country's myths. The figures on the vases tell stories, acting as a kind of movie of their time. From these clues, archaeologists get a lot of information about the people who lived before us, and how their lives, thoughts, and actions led to the way we live now.

Like archaeologists, **paleontologists** dig up clues to the past, too. Paleontologists look for fossils, or the remains of living things from long ago, including humans, plants, and animals such as dinosaurs. Skeletons of animals tell paleontologists how large the animals were, and remains of plants give clues about what the animals ate. Paleontologists also study fossils to learn about conditions on Earth many, many years before there were humans.

What It Takes

Becoming an archaeologist takes years of study and working in the field, assisting on digs. Oddly enough, most archaeologists don't major in archaeology when they go to college. Many major in anthropology, which is the study of human beings and their culture.

Because studying the ancient fossil bones of animals and humans is part of the job, students study anatomy.

Students still learn about archaeology in college, though, partly in the classroom and partly from helping on digs. That way, they learn how professional archaeologists work and how they approach problems.

To become a genuine archaeologist and lead digs, you need a master's degree. Usually that involves going to a "field school" for four to six weeks, often living in tents, and learning about the tools of the trade and how to dig.

Anna Roosevelt has dived into rivers, crawled through jungles, and climbed rocky cliffs to reach the sites of her discoveries—a long way from the lab!

What traits are useful for an archaeologist? "It's useful to like work, especially physical work," says Anna C. Roosevelt. She is an archaeologist who teaches at the University of Illinois. "I find it helpful that I like to search for things. Not finding things at first is not a problem for me. Rather, it makes me search harder. Persistence is a good trait, and optimism. The optimism draws you on to the goal you are after."

About her background, Roosevelt says, "My undergrad major was history with **minors** in classics and anthropology. My graduate school major was archaeology and human ecology in South America." She adds that in the 1980s and early 1990s, "I worked in Amazonia, mostly in Brazil and Venezuela, with short research visits to Peru and French Guiana. In the late 1990s and in the 2000s, I began to work in Central Africa, with several seasons in the Central African Republic and short research trips to the Congo and Rwanda."

For archaeologists, Roosevelt says, "it's useful not to be easily discouraged, since goals often take more time and work to reach than you expect. Because **innovative** researchers are eventually rewarded, it's important not to pay too much attention to negative comments about your work in progress. It's also useful not to turn back from the process of research if it does not turn out as you expect. It's good to be able

After the artifacts are returned from the field to the lab or museum, archaeologists make careful measurements to understand more fully their finds. Each find adds another piece to the puzzle of the past.

to use the research process to discover new things that you had not expected. If you are stuck on your original interpretation, you may not be able to discover something different and perhaps more interesting than what you originally thought."

Alana Cordy-Collins agrees. As an archaeologist, she says, you may have one idea about what you want to find, "only to find something totally unexpected that requires a total change of direction." One year, she says, her team planned to explore an area for its architecture, "but in setting up our tool shed, we found a cemetery. The architecture was less likely to be disturbed by looters than the burials, so we excavated the cemetery and learned things we hadn't yet asked."

Deborah Darnell, an archaeologist with Yale University, says that the most important trait for an archaeologist is: "You must really, really love the work for its own sake."

Being able to put up with whatever local conditions you find is also important. On a dig, an archaeologist might live out of a tent for a month or more, often in very hot or dry weather. Learning to make

Long days in the hot sun or hours spent crawling around in the dust are no big deal for archaeologists.

19

Archaeologists travel the world in search of clues to ancient civilizations. Some digs are in remote areas. Others, such as this one, are in the middle of busy cities such as Rome, Italy.

a safe camp, cook food outdoors, and stay clean and focused far from "civilization" will help any archaeologist. A person aiming for this sort of career should have a love of adventure . . . and of being outdoors.

International travel is also often a part of this work. To explore ancient cultures, scientists need to actually go to those places. Archaeological digs have taken place on every continent except Antarctica. Important discoveries were made in Africa about the origins of human beings. Throughout Europe, archaeologists have traced the spread and growth of civilizations. In Asia, the often-changing populations of peoples of the past have been explored in digs revealing royal courts and everyday lives.

Hard work, life in the outdoors, and a passport filled with travel stamps all await anyone exploring a career in archaeology.

Text-Dependent Questions

1. Why is being persistent important for an archaeologist?

2. What form of pottery is studied to learn about ancient Greek culture?

3. Name one place that Anna Roosevelt worked in the field.

Research Project

What part of the world are you curious about? Find out what ancient civilizations lived in that area. Can you find stories about digs or discoveries from that civilization? From how far back in time have human-made objects been found there?

Tools of the Trade

2

Unlike many scientists, archaeologists literally use tools. On a dig, they'll put out shovels, trowels, hammers, and picks. Being an archaeologist means working with your hands every day, whether clearing away pounds of dirt or shaving away tiny particles of ancient dust. Understanding the science behind ancient objects is a key technique, and archaeologists also make important discoveries using gear in their labs.

WORDS TO UNDERSTAND

artifacts   physical objects left behind by ancient people

atoms   tiny particles that make up matter

plumb bob   a heavy weight used in surveying or measuring to ensure a straight vertical line; the bob at the end of a string forms a line perpendicular to the ground

ratio   the amount of something compared to something else

A Different Kind of "Painting"

*I*f you've ever painted a picture, you probably know that big brushes are better for covering large areas of the paper or canvas quickly, and smaller brushes are better for putting in little details without smudging paint on everything else.

You can think of being an archaeologist as painting a picture of the past. Like painters, archaeologists have different tools to do their "painting," some of them bigger than others.

Uncovering a simple skull might take days, as the scientist pushes away sand almost a grain at a time.

The "big brushes" are the shovels used by archaeologists in the field to remove large amounts of soil as quickly as possible. The shoveled dirt is placed in large buckets, which hold five gallons or so. The dirt is then placed on screens. When the screens are shaken, the lighter soil falls through. Any **artifacts** are left on top, as they are too big to fall through the mesh of the screen.

While shovels speed up the job of finding objects that are in or under the soil, different tools are needed to avoid breaking those objects once they're found. People on digs

Clearing a dig site of the top layers of hard-packed dirt sometimes calls for heavier tools, and quite a bit of elbow grease. Being in good shape is important for an archaeologist heading for a dig.

use the hand trowel—a small metal tool with a handle—to remove dirt surrounding the objects they want to study. Sometimes, for the most delicate jobs, the diggers use tongue depressors—the same kind doctors use to look at your throat.

Then there is the soil core, often the size of a bicycle pump or smaller. A soil core is a metal tube with a handle at the top that archaeologists push into the ground to draw out soil samples so they can see if there are any artifacts and to study the soil itself. Scientists can tell whether the soil came from people's activity or was brought by winds from somewhere else. Studying soil can also establish what the region's climate was in the past and how the ground was used.

One of the most common artifacts found at many digs are potsherds, or broken pieces of pottery. Ceramics often survive burial better than other things that might break apart over the centuries.

How Old Is It?

*W*hen the soil contains remains of living things, a key question is how old those things are. In archaeology, the ages of fossils are determined through radiocarbon dating, the most important tool for finding out when people, animals, and plants lived. It works this way: Cosmic rays enter the earth's atmosphere and interact with **atoms** to produce carbon-14 atoms. Those combine with oxygen to form carbon dioxide, which is absorbed by plants. People and animals that eat plants also take in carbon-14. In the bodies of living things, the **ratio** of normal carbon, or carbon-12, to carbon-14 is always the same. When a living thing dies, carbon-12 remains in its system, but carbon-14 decays. The level of decay indicates how long ago something died. By comparing the ratio of carbon-12 to carbon-14 in the fossil to the ratio in still-living things, scientists can find out the age of a fossil.

Before the invention of radiocarbon dating in the late 1940s, archaeologists used two main methods for figuring out when things had happened at the sites they investigated. One was historical dating, based on written evidence from the past. The other was relative dating. For relative dating, investigators might study the way one type of soil was layered over another. Or they might group objects together that shared the same materials, shapes, or decorations, figuring that they

This machine examines the carbon atoms of pieces of artifacts. By reading the decay of those atoms, it can provide an accurate estimate of the age of the artifact.

were made at roughly the same time. Together with other evidence from the area, those findings helped to establish the ages of objects and remains. Radiocarbon dating, however, has proven to be much more accurate and has helped archaeologists zoom even closer to the true age of objects and relics.

At the Site

An archaeologist uses tools to mark, measure, and map the sites of a dig. String is used to mark the boundaries of a site. Line levels are attached to the string to keep it straight and keep the measurements accurate. To find out how deep a site is, a **plumb bob** is attached to a tape measure to pull it tight and straight for an accurate recording.

There are also more sophisticated tools for measuring how far things at an archaeological site are from one another, and for measuring their angles in relation to one another. A Total Station is useful for this work. For stability, a Total Station is usually mounted on a tripod. It sends out an electromagnetic signal, which bounces off a reflector and back to the Total Station. The Total Station then accurately measures the time it took the signal to bounce back. Based on the time, it can tell the distance, making for a reliable map of the site.

Look! Up in the Sky!

Since most archaeological work takes place on (and under) the ground, it may seem surprising that one important tool in this work is an airplane. Photographs taken from airplanes can reveal a lot about an area that is not visible on the ground. For example, plants can be tall or short, lush or sparse, depending on what is under the soil in which they grow. In areas that are on top of buried walls or other large pieces of hidden stone construction, soil is thinner and not as good, making for plants that do not grow as well as others. So, soil that is poor in quality may be rich in archaeological treasures. Therefore, if an aerial photograph shows patches of sparse or stunted plant life, it may be because there are very interesting things underneath.

Under the Sea

*M*ost archaeological work takes place on land, but there are also discoveries to be made on the ground at the bottom of oceans. That's where marine archaeologists come in. These specialists use many of the

Drones on Digs

Besides airplanes, other airborne tools are useful for locating where digs should take place. Drones, or unmanned aircraft, often have been used in modern warfare, but they can also have a more peaceful function. With heat-sensitive cameras attached, drones can reveal walls, buildings, or other structures buried beneath surfaces. In recent years, that equipment has been used to investigate in a matter of hours what would previously have taken months or longer. In addition, drones have accomplished the task without harming the artifacts.

same tools that are used on the ground, but underwater tools are made of plastic so they will not be destroyed by salt water. Also, instead of using shovels to dig dirt that is then placed in buckets and carried to screens, underwater archaeologists employ dredge engines with 100-foot (30-m) pumps. Moving 600 gallons (2,271 l) of water per minute, these engines bring up sediment, depositing it on fine-meshed floating screens that catch even tiny artifacts. This equipment is vital for investigating sites of shipwrecks, for example.

With holes in the earth, long trenches, or deep pits, dig sites can be hazardous. Often the site is in a very hard-to-reach place, too. Hard hats are not unusual, along with sturdy clothing and boots.

Almost all marine archaeologists are expert divers, able to spend many hours beneath the water, searching and digging. They also need to be able to live on ships for many weeks at a time, as their "floating laboratory" anchors above a dig site. Sometimes, just getting to and from such a place means battling storms and rough weather.

What's That You're Wearing?

Just as the tools archaeologists use are important, so are the clothes they wear. In general, archaeologists wear clothes that are comfortable and durable: long pants to protect their knees when they kneel in the dirt, and soft leather shoes that protect their feet but are not so heavy that they accidentally ruin artifacts. They wear long sleeves and wide-brimmed hats to protect them from the sun. Cargo pants—with lots of pockets—are especially handy for holding tools such as notebooks, pencils, and trowels. For objects too big to be carried in pants pockets, such as cameras or water bottles, archaeologists bring along satchels or backpacks. Some archaeologists wear gloves to protect their hands while digging; others prefer not to, so they can enjoy the feel of the soil.

 # Text-Dependent Questions

1. Name the process that uses carbon-14 to date artifacts.
2. What kind of archaeologist works underwater?
3. Why is "painting" part of archaeology?

 # Research Project

If you get the okay from your parents or school, set up a small dig site in your yard or schoolyard. Mark out an area three yards (2.7 m) on each side with string. Then dig away the soil until you discover something made by people. It might not be that old, but you'll get the same feeling of discovery an archaeologist gets. In some parts of North America, you even might stumble on artifacts from long-ago Native Americans or early American settlers.

Tales From the Field!

Even in times that we now think of as ancient, people sometimes found fascinating things from even earlier times. In the 6th century BCE, a Babylonian king named Nabonidus dug beneath the floor of a temple and found a stone foundation that had been put down thousands of years before he lived. In the time of the Roman Empire, soldiers under Julius Caesar's rule found very old tombs and pots as they set up colonies in Italy and Greece.

Some of the more recent finds in archaeology have made headlines around the world. Others have been less famous, but have contributed greatly to our understanding of the people and civilizations that came before us.

WORDS TO UNDERSTAND

hominids   early human-like ancestors of today's human beings

metal detectors   devices that use magnetic waves to locate buried metal objects

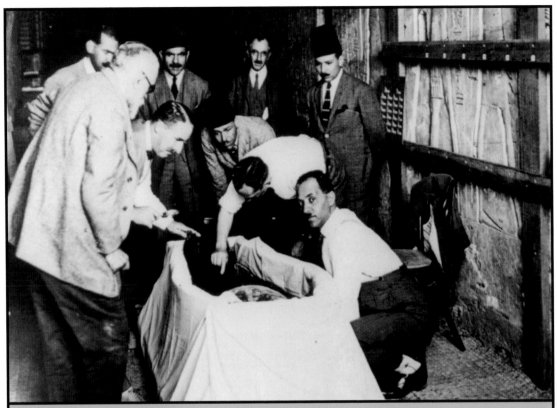

The British archaeologist Howard Carter, leaning in from the left of the photo, shocked the world and opened up a new world of exploration with his discovery of King Tut's tomb in 1922.

King Tut

The most famous archaeological find of all time is probably that of the Egyptian boy king Tutankhamen. He lived more than 3,000 years ago and is best known as King Tut. The tomb and remains of King Tut were hard to find. The ancient Egyptians planned it that way. Because Egyptians believed that they could take possessions with them to the next life when they died, they were often buried with jewels and other treasures. Thieves sometimes robbed the graves and stole those treasures. So Egyptian pharaohs began building their tombs in places they thought no one could find.

In 1738, when the Englishman Richard Pococke went to Egypt's Valley of the Kings, he discovered just how hard the tombs were to locate. He and his party traveled miles through narrow valleys between mountains, heading down skinny passages carved through rock, before finding tombs—and even those tombs had been robbed! The famous Italian-born archaeologist Giovanni Batista Belzoni also went to the Valley of the Kings, but he, too, found tombs that had been robbed centuries earlier.

Then, in 1922, another Englishman, Howard Carter, had better luck. He and his assistants discovered what turned out to be the tomb of Tutankhamen. King Tut died while he was still a teenager. Although he was not very important as Egyptian rulers ago, he made a great archaeological find.

After Carter's team found the tomb, he sent a telegram to England asking his sponsor, Lord Carnavon, to come for the opening. As the pair breached the final wall, Carnavon asked Carter what he saw. "Wonderful things," answered Carter in what became a famous saying.

Carter pulled the sarcophagus, or burial coffin, of Tut, along with dozens of artifacts of gold and other precious metals. From this, he was able to learn a great amount about how the Egyptians buried their dead. Picture writing on the walls and objects told the story of the boy king. In the years following the find, rumors of a "curse" on the mummy were often talked about, with believers claiming many of the people present at the opening had died. Scientists, however, believe in facts, not curses.

King Tut's remains and treasures drew large crowds in many cities when they toured the United States in the 1970s. They remain popular in museums in Cairo, Egypt, and still go on display in other places around the world.

Troy Was Real

*A*nother very important archaeological find occurred in the 1860s. Many things that people once believed (for example, that the Earth is flat) were later found to be untrue, but the amazing thing about this archaeological discovery was that it did the opposite. It proved that a place once thought to be imaginary was actually real! It all started with the Greek poet Homer, who lived in the 7th or 8th century BCE. Homer is famous for two long story-poems, *The Iliad* and *The Odyssey*. *The Iliad* is about the Trojan War. According to Homer's story, the war was fought after the warrior Paris, who was from Troy, took Helen away from her husband, Menelaus, king of Sparta in ancient Greece. A group of Greek states then attacked Troy, setting off a war that lasted for ten years. *The Iliad* includes some of the most famous characters in all of literature, such as Hector, Agamemnon, Odysseus, Nestor, and Achilles.

For many years, scholars believed that Troy was not a real city. However, a German man named Heinrich Schliemann, who was raised in the 1840s on tales of the Trojan War, never doubted that Troy was real. As an adult, he set out to find it. His reading and investigating led him to Turkey. At first Schliemann was not as careful as today's archaeologists are. In his search for evidence of Troy, he worked very quickly and probably destroyed a lot of valuable remains. Then a young man on his staff, Wilhelm Dorpfeld, persuaded Schliemann that he should work more slowly and carefully. Schliemann faced great challenges in his dig, such as huge blocks of stone in the way of his work. The men with him had to stop what they were doing to move the stone. The work paid off, and Schliemann uncovered thousands of artifacts used

Visitors to this former dig site in Turkey can walk on the streets of the ancient city of Troy. Connecting the present to the past is a major part of the appeal of archaeology.

in ancient times. He had found the real city of Troy! (As for the story of the Trojan War, many now believe that it was created from details of other wars and battles.)

Uphill Battle

Some of the fiercest and bloodiest military battles in history took place during the Punic Wars. Fought between 264 and 146 BCE, these three confrontations pitted Rome against the forces of Carthage's Punic Empire. Each side tried to win control of the Mediterranean Sea. The ancient historians Polybius and Livy wrote famous accounts of the wars, and for more than 2,000 years, generations had only their word for what happened.

Then, just a few years ago, with Polybius and Livy's descriptions of the battlefields as guides, two archaeologists from Spain used satellite and Internet technology to find the scene of the hard-fought Battle of Baecula that took place in 208 BCE. Polybius wrote that the army of the Carthaginian leader Hasdrubal camped on a hill with a river behind it and flat ground in front. Livy added that the level ground was at the top of the hill and was surrounded on three sides by ridges of hills. In the early 2000s, Arturo Ruiz and Juan Pedro Bellón looked at maps and Google Earth to examine hundreds of miles of ground, to find a site that looked like the one the historians described. They narrowed the search down to 20 places, then searched them with **metal detectors**, looking for weapons. In 2004, on top of a hill in the Spanish village of Santo Tomé, the metal detectors started to beep!

Just four inches (10 cm) below the ground's surface, Ruiz and Bellón found remains of all kinds of weapons: spears, arrowheads, daggers, and more. Expanding their search over the years, the archaeologists have discovered almost 700 nails from shoes worn by the Roman soldiers. From the locations of the nails, Ruiz and Bellón realized that the Romans led by Scipio and Laelius had charged up the hills to attack the Carthaginians, just as Polybius and Livy had written! According to the historians, the Carthaginians used all kinds of weapons against the Romans as they climbed the hills, including the spears, arrows, and darts Ruiz and Bellón had found. Still, the Romans made it to the top, where they easily defeated the Carthaginians. According to Livy, about 8,000 Carthaginians were killed. With 21st-century technology, the archaeologists found evidence of a battle people had previously known about only from books.

The modern city of Santo Tomé, Spain, was the site of a battle during Roman times, more than 2,400 years ago. Archaeologists found evidence of that battle in the fields surrounding the city.

Shipwreck!

*T*echnology helped archaeologists find remains on top of a hill. It can do the same under the sea. When companies drill for oil offshore (that is, in the water), the Bureau of Ocean Energy Management requires them to be on the lookout for historical remains. One day in 2011, in the Gulf of Mexico, the Shell Oil Company spotted the wreck of a ship that the bureau decided to call *Monterrey A*.

Helping the company to find out about this ancient ship was an underwater robot, Hercules, equipped with two mechanical arms, suction cups, and a small vacuum. Working just above the ocean floor, Hercules was attached by thousands of feet of cables to a sea vessel called *Nautilus*. Inside *Nautilus* were Brendan Phillips and James Delgado. While Phillips helped steer Hercules from the water's surface, Delgado, a marine archaeologist, sat in front of video screens showing Hercules's activities, and he communicated with others about what the robot was doing. The "others" included a group of fellow scientists, plus thousands of people watching from all over the world. While archaeologists working on land do the actual digging, marine archaeologists rely on submersibles or even scuba divers. In this case, the site was too deep for divers, so Hercules was the perfect tool.

The *Monterrey A* was 84 feet (25.6 m) long. As Hercules went about its work, Delgado and others judged from the cannons, anchors, bottles, and navigational devices they could see that the wrecked ship was from the 19th century. Delgado figured out that the crew of the *Monterrey A* did not abandon the ship, or else they would have taken the devices with them onto a smaller boat. In other words, the crew probably went down with the ship.

Blackbeard Sails Again!

One of the most famous pirates in history was Blackbeard, an Englishman who raided along the coast of the colonial United States. He was killed in 1718 by British Navy sailors during a battle near North Carolina. Blackbeard's main ship, *Queen Anne's Revenge*, had been sunk earlier, but no one was sure where. In 1996, after searching for many years, archaeologists found the wreckage of a ship of that era in the water off the North Carolina shore. In 2011—after studying thousands of artifacts, including cannons, gold, and even plates and cups from the pirates' tables—they confirmed that it was the famous pirate ship.

Keep Trying

When you want to accomplish something, it pays to keep trying. Being brave helps, too. Nobody has proved that better than Michel Brunet, a French paleontologist. Brunet began his career by studying ancient hoofed animals. One day, though, he decided that since he was human, he wanted to know where humans came from. Who were the earliest human ancestors?

Brunet went in search of remains of **hominids**, the group that includes humans as well as our extinct ancestors. Beginning when Mary Leakey found a hominid bone in Tanzania in 1959, it was thought that the first hominids came from the eastern part of Africa. Brunet decided to see if he could find their remains in other places. This was sometimes dangerous work. Once, while he was looking for hominid remains in the war-torn country of Afghanistan, a low-flying fighter jet fired at Brunet and his team. Fortunately, the pilot missed. Another time, in Iraq, Brunet was arrested. A short time later he was released. Why was he arrested? He never found out.

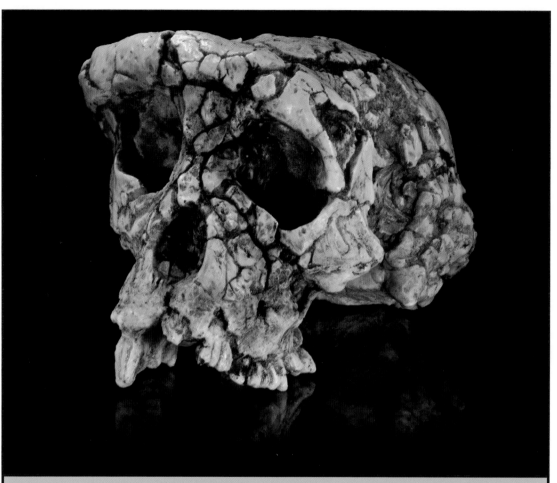

Archaeologists need patience. The French scientist Michel Brunet searched for more than 20 years for further evidence of early man. This re-assembled skull was part from a dig in Africa was the end result.

Later, Brunet started to look for hominids in parts of the African continent besides east Africa. He and others with him had to raise money for their search from a lot of different sources. They spent years looking for hominids in the African country of Cameroon, but didn't find any. Because he failed, he had trouble getting more money. Not only that, but in 1989 Abel Brillanceau, a good friend of Brunet's who was working him, died of malaria, a disease spread by mosquitoes. Brunet was crushed, but he didn't give up.

Then, in 1993, the government of Chad, in north-central Africa, invited Brunet to try his search for hominids there. The fierce desert winds there could sometimes make it hard to work, but once in a while they helped uncover valuable artifacts. In January 1995 in Chad, Brunet found a hominid jawbone that was 3.5 million years old. He named it Abel, after his dead friend. Six-and-a-half years later, a member of Brunet's team in Chad found a whole hominid cranium. Many believe it to be between six and seven million years old. That would make the hominid it belonged to the oldest known human ancestor. Brunet's perseverance had paid off!

 **Text-Dependent Questions**

1. Where was "Tut hunter" Howard Carter from?
2. What did archaeologists use to find a shipwreck?
3. Name the Greek poet who wrote *The Iliad*.

Research Project

A bit of history detective work: Pick an era of history that particularly interests you. Now find out what archaeologists have discovered about that time. Look for reports of digs or discoveries of artifacts. What do those artifacts reveal about the people of that era?

Scientists in the News

Major British Digger: Kathleen Kenyon (1906–1978) was an English archaeologist who unearthed materials from Jericho, in Jordan, and discovered that it is the oldest continuously lived-in city in the world. She found ancient artifacts in Britain and wrote about her discoveries there from the early 1930s to the early 1950s. Kenyon led archaeological expeditions in the Roman city of Sabratha in the late 1940s and early 1950s. She then served as principal of St. Hugh's College at Oxford for 11 years beginning in 1962, and she was made a Dame of the British Empire in 1973. It was during her time as director of the British School of Archaeology in Jerusalem, from 1951 to 1966, that Kenyon made her most famous discovery. In the city of Jericho, which is mentioned in the Old Testament of the Bible, she found evidence that people farmed for a living as early as 7000 BCE, or 9,000 years ago.

Groundbreakers . . . in More Ways Than One: The Leakeys are often called the "First Family of Archaeology." Through their work in Tanzania, the Leakeys established that the earliest human ancestors lived in Africa. Their later findings revealed that ancestors there had walked upright more than three million years ago. They also discovered possibly the first relatives of humans to work with tools, two million years in the past. Louis Leakey (1903–1972) was born in

Kenya, in Africa, where his parents were missionaries. Finding ancient stone tools near the river when he was growing up helped shape his career choice. He went to Olduvai Gorge (in what is now Tanzania) for the first time in 1931 and made significant dis-

Mary and Louis Leakey made many important discoveries.

/ Douglas
), Richard
o work in
n a hom-
out to be
rs, Mary discovered footprints of
fossils found in the same region.
et. That proved that walking up-
tors than brain growth or modern
Jonathan and Richard; Richard's
uise, carry on their work.

sh archaeologists found someone
an 500 years: King Richard III of
ground garage in Leicester found
ed in and started digging further.
that they might have found the
5. They used DNA from the bones
elatives. The DNA matched, and
the king made headlines around
were reburied in a church grave-
ry.

Find Out More

Books

Adams, Amanda. *Ladies of the Fields: Early Women Archaeologists and Their Search for Adventure.* Vancouver: Greystone Books, 2010.

Fagan, Brian M. (editor). *The Great Archaeologists.*
New York: Thames & Hudson, 2014.

Steele, Philip. *Eyewitness Books: Treasure.* New York: DK Publishing, 2010.

Yeager, C.G. *Arrowheads and Stone Artifacts: A Practical Guide for the Amateur Archaeologist.* Portland, Oregon: WestWinds Press, 2010.

Web Sites

Archaeology Magazine www.archaeology.org
The official publication site of the Archaeological Institute of America is packed with news and features on the latest finds.

National Geographic news.nationalgeographic.com/news/archives/ancient-world/
National Geographic magazine creates this site to document new discoveries from around the world.

National Park Service www.cr.nps.gov/archeology/
Combine visits to National Parks with archaeological investigations!

Series Glossary of Key Terms

airlock   a room on a space station from which astronauts can move from inside to outside the station and back

anatomy   a branch of knowledge that deals with the structure of organisms

bionic   to be assisted by mechanical movements

carbon dioxide   a gas that is in the air that we breathe out

classified   kept secret from all but a few people in a government or an organization

deforestation   the destruction of forest or woodland

diagnose   to recognize by signs and symptoms

discipline   in science, this means a particular field of study

elite   the part or group having the highest quality or importance

genes   information stored in cells that determine a person's physical characteristics

geostationary   remaining in the same place above the Earth during an orbit

innovative   groundbreaking, original

inquisitiveness   an ability to be curious, to continue asking questions to learn more

internships   jobs often done for free by people in the early stages of study for a career

marine   having to do with the ocean

meteorologist   a scientist who forecasts weather and weather patterns

physicist   a scientist who studies physics, which examines how matter and energy move and relate

primate   a type of four-limbed mammal with a developed brain; includes humans, apes, and monkeys

traits   a particular quality or personality belonging to a person

Index

Photo Credits

About the Author

Clifford Thompson is the former editor in chief of *Current Biography*, a monthly magazine and annual book. In 2014, he received a Whiting Writers' Award for nonfiction for his book *Love for Sale and Other Essays*. He lives in Brooklyn, N.Y.